I0579537

The ART of
NAPKIN FOLDING

The ART of NAPKIN FOLDING

includes 20 step-by-step napkin folds plus finishing touches
for the perfect table setting

RYLAND PETERS & SMALL
LONDON • NEW YORK

Senior designer Toni Kay
Editor Miriam Catley
Production David Hearn
Art director Leslie Harrington
Editorial director Julia Charles
Publisher Cindy Richards

First published in 2012
This revised edition published in 2018 by
Ryland Peters & Small
20–21 Jockey's Fields
London WC1R 4BW
and
341 E 116th St
New York NY 10029

www.rylandpeters.com

Text copyright © Liz Belton, Margaret
Caselton, Rebecca Tanqueray and
Ryland Peters & Small 2012, 2018
Design and photographs
© Ryland Peters & Small 2012, 2018

10 9 8 7 6 5 4 3 2 1

All rights reserved. No part of this
publication may be reproduced, stored in a
retrieval system or transmitted in any form
or by any means, electronic, mechanical,
photocopying or otherwise, without the
prior permission of the publisher.

A CIP record for this book is available from
the British Library.

US Library of Congress cataloging-in-
publication data has been applied for.

ISBN 978-1-84975-974-8

Printed and bound in China.

contents

introduction

The napkin is as practical and useful an object as anything else on the table, but it can also be the most decorative element. No table setting is complete without this vital ingredient. Tableware need not match to look effective – table linens can be dainty or dramatic, or you can use a traditional large damask napkin for special occasions. This book aims to encourage and inspire anyone wanting to create an inviting table setting.

napkins in history

The history of the napkin is a long and most interesting one. Indeed, one anonymous French researcher has taken the subject so seriously that he or she refers to the 1960s and '70s as the era of 'emancipation' – of the napkin and table setting, rather than conventional morality!

There is without doubt an emancipation in the rigours of table etiquette from the early 20th century, when only 'double damask' would do and Emily Post, author of *Etiquette: The Blue Book of Social Usage*, pronounced that 'napkins should never… be put on the side, because it looks as though you are showing off the beauty of your place plate' or 'very fancy foldings are not in good taste', and every household dutifully obeyed. Meal times could not have been much fun when everyone was looking out to check that every affectation of manners was being observed.

Today there are no such rules, apart from those of consideration and courtesy. At dinner parties, the trend is towards creating a pleasant ambience with the table settings and lighting. The emphasis is on making guests feel welcome by creating a convivial atmosphere. This can be helped with a well-planned table setting. Place cards, fun napkin folds, fresh flowers or herbs tucked into napkins, and pretty or personalized napkin rings will all create talking points, make guests feel that you have taken care, help the party get started and, above all, make them feel as if a fine feast is about to take place. Contemporary etiquette, according to Drusilla Beyfus in her book *Modern Manners*, suggests that napkins can be laid either in the centre of a place setting or placed on the side plate. The only golden rule, she says, is that 'whatever its design, a napkin should always look and feel freshly laundered'.

It is believed that the ancient Romans introduced napkins. Two were used: one large napkin was tied around the neck, and slaves would pour perfumed water over the guests' hands and dry them with a second napkin. It was during the Middle Ages that table linen became fashionable, and by the 16th century most of the wealthier households would lay the table for meals. People at that time ate with their fingers and a knife, and either wiped their hands on the tablecloth or on their bread. Therefore, the tablecloth was changed several times during the meal, and sometimes two or three cloths were laid one over the other. (In some restaurants, a change of cloth during the meal is still a custom.) Another method was to lay a border or 'cover' of linen over the edge of the table, which is the origin of the restaurant 'cover' charge.

double damask
(opposite above) A double damask napkin in a silver napkin ring indicates a formal table setting. In the Middle Ages, the size of the napkin would have indicated the rank of the guest.

starched linen (right)
Starched napkins are piled high in preparation for a dinner. In earlier times, when large households employed a team of staff, there were servants whose exclusive job it was to care for the linen.

formal place setting *This formal place setting has a white damask napkin and cutlery for two courses. Napkins are usually placed on top of the dinner plate or, alternatively, on the left-hand side of the setting.*

Historically, the size of napkin that a guest brought to a meal would signify his wealth, therefore, the larger the napkin, the wealthier the guest. Servants would tie the napkin around the neck like a bib, and if the napkin was on the small size, it was said that its owner could 'just make ends meet'. Napkins belonging to the *seigneur*, or lord of the manor, were large and luxurious and often magnificently embroidered. They were draped over the diner's arm, just as a waiter in a smart restaurant might carry a napkin today – a habit that may have developed from this ancient custom.

Napkins have followed the dictates of fashion. In the times of ruffs and large lace collars, napkins were enormous in order to cover these elaborate accessories. As fashions changed, so did the style of the napkin, and by the early 19th century the way in which it was used became a subject of scrutiny. Today, we only use napkins to dab our mouths or wipe our fingers.

In the 17th century, particularly in France, there was a vogue for folded napkins. One can imagine the theatre of special celebrations when napkins were folded into the shapes of animals, fruit, birds, butterflies and other complex shapes. Napkin folding was a profession in itself and a 'napkin folder' was employed by wealthy households to arrive the day before a feast and create these displays. This gave meals and banquets a great sense of occasion and it is this feeling of visual excitement that we can recreate at our own table, using the plethora of different napkins and accessories we have at our disposal.

informal setting *An informal setting requires only enough cutlery / flatware for one course – the knife and fork may be placed together on top of the napkin, on the right-hand side of the diner's plate.*

age-old traditions *At formal restaurants or grand dinners, a starched white napkin is often placed over the waiter's arm; a tradition that may have its origins back in the Middle Ages.*

practical and elegant *Napkins are sometimes placed around the neck of a wine bottle once it has been opened, to prevent drips or splashing when wine is poured, and to soak up any condensation if the wine is chilled.*

sizes and types of napkin

Table linen, just like clothes, has its changing fashions and today we enjoy
a wonderful choice of napkins, ranging from the correctly formal to the
purely whimsical and decorative. There is always a suitable napkin for every
type of function, from banquets and weddings, luncheons and afternoon
teas and cocktail parties to more casual gatherings of friends and family.

The type of napkin used usually denotes the level
of formality or the spirit of the occasion. Since
the 17th century, it has been traditional for large
white or cream damask, or plain-woven napkins
to be used on formal dinner or lunch occasions.

One of the finest dinner napkins is the 'double
damask'. Damask is a firm fabric woven on a
jacquard loom. Traditionally made of silk from
Damascus, it can now be made from cotton,
wool or a combination of fibres. The richly
figurative design is produced by the contrast of
a sateen weft against a satin warp. On a double
damask, the pattern is represented on both sides
of the napkin. Linen is preferable to cotton, as
it is resistant to sunlight and is stronger.

luxurious linen *(top left) A 'double damask' dinner
napkin is the most luxurious and elegant option.*

the perfect fit *(bottom left) This classic setting
demonstrates the simple arrangement of a folded
damask napkin just overlapping the top and bottom
of the dinner plate.*

There are only general rules as to the correct size of a napkin. Traditionally, dinner napkins vary in size from 75 cm/30 inches square to 50 cm/20 inches. Anything smaller than this would be considered a lunch or supper napkin. Luncheon napkins tend to be more decorative and less formal than those used for dinner. Many feature embroidery or other decoration, such as drawn thread work or a woven or printed border.

Afternoon tea napkins are smaller still, at roughly 30–20 cm/12–8 inches square, and can but don't have to be laid on the lap. In the 19th and early 20th centuries, afternoon tea napkins were often exquisitely embroidered. Tiny cocktail or finger napkins are often fashioned from less sturdy, more fashionable fabrics. These can be made from lace, organza and organdie or fine cotton lawn. Cocktail napkins range from 15 cm/6 inches square down to handkerchief size.

various napkin sizes *(above) from top to bottom: cocktail, tea, lunch, dinner and traditional early 20th-century French napkins.*

fine linen *(below left) An inviting afternoon tea tray is set with a white tray cloth and fine linen and organza appliquéd napkins.*

cocktail napkins *(far right) Champagne and strawberries are perfect for a summer's day, and fine Swiss linen scalloped-edged and embroidered cocktail napkins make a charming accompaniment. Settings can be enhanced by linking the napkin decoration to that on the china or glassware. Here, the curves on the napkin echo the more graphic curves on the Christian Lacroix tea plate.*

less is more *A modern and minimalist place card has been created using string and stencilled card to match a contemporary-style setting. The leaf pattern on the card echoes the other natural elements used for this table.*

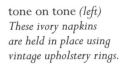

tone on tone *(left)*
These ivory napkins
are held in place using
vintage upholstery rings.

cross stitch *(right)*
Create a stylish tie using
a strip of felt sealed with
two neat cross stitches.

rope braid *(above)* *A coiled satin rope braid*
napkin ring gives textural interest and adds to the
contemporary use of materials in this elegant setting.

ties and ribbons

There are so many different ways in
which we can use napkins to decorate
and embellish table settings. Sometimes
a napkin decorated with a simple tie or
ribbon is all you need to add a stylish
finishing touch to your table. Napkins
may be tied with a wide variety of
materials. Bracelets, necklaces, beads
and haberdashery trimmings can all
create beautiful and unique effects.
Mixing colours, textures and fabrics
is a great way to create different looks.

beautiful beads *(above left)* *Long wooden beads are*
tied onto strips of leather and used as a simple napkin tie.

colours and textures *(above right)* *Gold and green*
make the perfect match for an autumnal dinner setting.

natural decoration

Take advantage of what nature has to offer in every season. Snip a small cluster of roses or foliage from the garden, gather glossy nuts from the autumn harvest or, if you do not have a garden, use small fruits or fresh herbs from the supermarket. Beachcombing provides a cornucopia of goodies such as shells, sea-smoothed pebbles and small, unusual shapes of driftwood.

Napkins can be used to wrap tiny potted plants at each place setting. Fold the napkin into a triangle and tie it around the pot using a contrasting ribbon or cord. Your guests can simply untie the napkin for use before the meal. Miniature pots of flowers are plentiful in spring and summer, and small-headed garden flowers such as lavender, pansies, daisies, pinks, violets or patio roses are all ideal.

Another idea is to pot up fresh herbs such as basil and thyme, which can then be used as a garnish for the meal. Little pots of spearmint or lemon verbena are also useful — guests can use the leaves to clean and scent their hands if they have been eating with their fingers.

flower power *(this page and opposite) Natural decorations are simple and effective: try vine leaves, a cluster of grapes, flower heads, shells, fresh herbs, small fruits, hazelnuts or even a dainty daisy chain.*

stripes and squares *(opposite) Create a striking table for an informal or family gathering using different patterned napkins in checks, stripes or pretty floral prints. Choose decorations that match your chosen napkins, such as bright flowers with a floral fabric or a piece of rope and a marine shackle to dress up a breezy, nautical-style striped cotton napkin.*

sharp design and bright colours *(left)*
checks and stripes are always fun.

bright and beautiful
(below far left) A set of bright linen napkins with faggoted hems creates a kaleidoscope of colour on a tabletop.

blue on blue *(below left) A collection of different tones and textures themed around one colour works well for big parties as well as everyday occasions. Blue is ideal for this treatment because the spectrum is so vast and varied.*

colours and patterns

Napkins aren't just for special occasions. Strong colours and bold patterns will brighten up any midweek meal. If you're having a casual supper for family or friends, you don't need to use formal napkin rings – instead, you can experiment with easy knots and casual folds. Make life simple by choosing natural fabrics that wash well and don't need too much ironing.

utility chic *(above)*
For everyday meals, choose no-frills, easy-wash linen that's functional and fun, such as checked cotton, waffle weave or pretty floral prints.

a splash of colour *Monogramming napkins with a bright colour creates a colourful and more informal look. Here, the sprig of vine leaves matches the green embroidery thread used on the napkin to create a fresh feel.*

traditional monogram *(below left and right)*
*Monogramming napkins adds an elegant touch for more
formal occasions. Crisp white napkins embroidered with
the first letter of the last name of each guest is traditional.*

creative embellishment *(above) Tiny mother-of-
pearl buttons with their distinctive mottled backing
have been sewn onto the corner of a marine blue
napkin. When adding decorations to napkins, remember
to confine them to one corner only so that the napkin
can still serve its purpose.*

embroidery and embellishment

Embroidered napkins and tablecloths were very popular
in Victorian and Edwardian times. Pretty pieces, often
with freehand characterful embroidery, are still plentiful
and can be found at antiques fairs, second-hand stores,
online auction websites and street markets. Monogramming
is the classic form of ornamentation on napkins; a
monogram stitched in white thread on white fabric has
its own timeless elegance. Adding an embroidered initial
is a good way to personalize a napkin for a gift.

pretty florals *Embroidered
daisies on a pure white linen
napkin bring a light springtime
touch to a lunchtime table setting.*

setting the scene

The style of a table setting can be used as a guide to the formality or spirit of an occasion. Ornately folded linen or damask napkins look right for formal events such as a dinner or wedding, while more casual entertaining scenarios offer an opportunity for playful settings with a variety of napkins in different sizes, patterns and colours.

perfect pastels *Use simply folded linen napkins in pretty pastel colours to match your tablecoth. Using gift labels to create place cards is another way to add a personal touch. A casual but beautifully decorated table means less work for you and makes everyone feel relaxed.*

colour match *(left)*
Taking a minute to consider the colour combinations of a table setting can make all the difference. Choosing complementary shades, such as these subtle pinks and greens, works well, especially for a casual springtime occasion.

pretty paper *(below)*
Paper napkins are available in countless designs today and are perfect for eating outside or if you have little ones around who like to get messy. Choose a bright pattern in keeping with the overall theme.

country flowers

For an informal spring or summer get-together with friends, a light floral theme will go down a treat. Pinks and blues are the obvious colour choices, but don't overdo it or you'll tip the balance from sweet to saccharine. Keep the overall look soft and pretty, and stick to simple accessories and plenty of fresh flowers. This theme would be perfect for a baby shower, a Mother's Day lunch or a christening meal.

perfect patterns *(above) A faded floral print complements the geometric pattern on the tableware. Simple cutlery with blue handles completes this clean, modern look.*

fine china *(left) A simple white napkin embroidered with a floral pattern is the perfect partner for fine bone china.*

a touch of sparkle *(opposite) For a bolder version of this theme, use patterned, brightly coloured tableware with embroidered napkins to match. Here, a floral, beaded bracelet has been used to create a stylish napkin ring to complement the pretty vintage plates.*

Napkins and table linen with floral designs are an essential part of this fun, pretty theme. From bold prints to simple, understated white cotton with a flower embroidered in one corner, there is something to suit many different styles. First choose a tablecloth or fold a piece of fabric to fit your table. Don't restrict yourself to plain white – a pastel-coloured or floral cloth can make a room feel cheerful. Then choose your napkins to match. Simple folds such as the 'rose' or the 'envelope' (shown on the following pages) would work best with this theme. Use plain tableware for a more modern feel, or fine china decorated with floral patterns for a decorative look. Finish the table with flowers in simple glass bottles and prepare some lovely things to eat.

one Fold an open, square napkin in half, bringing the bottom corner up to the top corner, seam-side in, to make a large triangle.

two Fold the bottom of the triangle up to make a large hem, about 5 cm/2 inches wide.

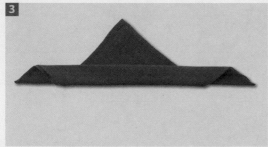
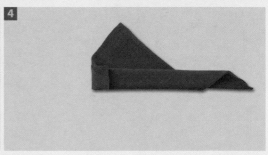

three Fold the hem up again, leaving a small triangle at the top.

four Beginning from the left-hand corner, roll the hem inwards from the left-hand side until you almost reach the opposite corner.

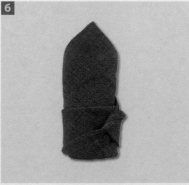

five Wind the corner around and tuck the end into the slanted edge at the base of the napkin.

six Turn the two top corners inside out to form the leaves around the base of the rose.

rose

Folding a plain-coloured linen napkin into an elegant 'rose' is guaranteed to impress your guests on any occasion. This beautiful fold will work perfectly with a floral-themed table, especially when using ornate, floral tableware. Plain fabrics work best for this fold, as a pattern would get lost in the spiral of the petals.

seven Turn the folded napkin over and shape the leaves of the rose as desired before placing the napkin in the centre of the plate.

envelope

A simple fold for a light lunch or informal supper, the 'envelope' does not require a starched napkin and is best fashioned from soft, supple fabrics that will drape well. Plain as well as pastel or floral napkins are most suitable for this fold — when folded, floral prints often create their own pleasing geometric pattern.

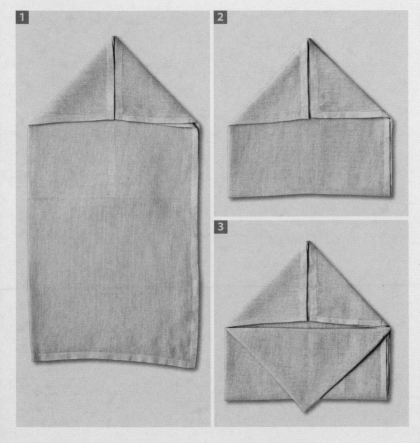

two Fold the lower half of the rectangle up to completely cover the pointed top half. For the second flap, fold down the corners of the top layer to meet in the same way as before to form another point over the top of the first one.

three Fold the top pointed layer down so that the tip of the point reaches just below the bottom edge. Make a crease along the fold with your thumb. Now fold down the second pointed flap over the first; don't crease this fold but leave it soft. Place the second flap slightly higher than the lower one so that the double layer of flaps is clearly visible.

one Fold the napkin in half to form a large rectangle, with a short end nearest you. To make the flap of the envelope, form a point at the top end of the rectangle by folding down each of the top corners towards the centre. Make sure the edges meet neatly.

natural elements

Here, the soft greens and browns of the table linen used form the basis of a smart, garden-themed table. Choose neutral colours and natural adornments such as these raffia-wrapped glasses, and wild grasses and sculptural seedheads in place of more conventional flowers.

natural selection *(opposite, all) Neutral colours and cool greens would work well for the linens and tableware for this theme. Napkins should be folded using folds such as the 'place card holder' (see overleaf) or simply tied with ribbons or garden twine that are in keeping with the colour scheme.*

take your place *(opposite, top right) Place cards work well when they tie in with the rest of the tabletop theme. To recreate the effect, buy ready-made cards or make your own using stencils or stamps. Punch a hole in one corner and tie the cards to linen napkins using garden twine or string.*

layer on texture *(above) Contrast the smooth metal of the cutlery with the roughness of stone for a rich and intriguing combination of textures.*

make it inviting *(left) Think of simple but innovative ways to lay the table that take it beyond the everyday. Here, linen runners have been laid across the table to create a chic modern settting.*

place card holder

This is a more complex fold that is worth the practice. The 'place card holder' is ideal for larger gatherings where place cards are necessary. This fold requires a large napkin, heavily starched to hold the tight rolls required, and is suited to pale tones and neutral colours.

one First make a narrrow rectangular strip by folding the bottom third of the napkin up and then the top third down over the lower third. Holding the centre point of the bottom edge with your finger, fold the left half of the strip diagonally upwards, and then the right half. Turn the napkin over from top to bottom so that the point is now at the top.

two Roll one of the lower flaps up tightly until it meets the fold. Hold it in place while you roll up the other flap.

three Turn the napkin over from top to bottom so that the point is now at the bottom once more and the two rolls are at the top. Fold the left-hand side down towards the bottom point so that the roll lines up with the central vertical fold. Fold the right-hand side down to the bottom point so that the two rolls line up alongside one another and the base forms a square. Slide your place card between the two rolls. The name should be written high enough on the card to be instantly visible.

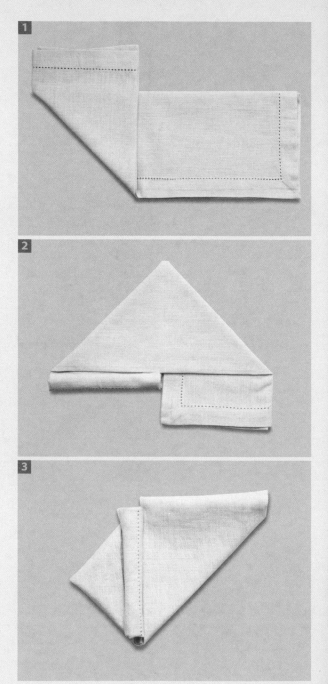

understated elegance *Smart and streamlined, this tabletop has a clubby, sophisticated feel. Keep the scheme understated and masculine with dark tones and polished textures. A glossy bare wood table is perfect, but if you don't have one, throw over a deep brown or green cloth, or a runner. Keep decorative trimmings to a minimum; a chic, uncluttered look is your aim.*

contemporary chic

With just a little effort you can transform your everyday table into the perfect backdrop for entertaining. You don't need to buy anything special; just opt for a smart and contemporary, pared-down look and add some personal touches: homemade placemats, perhaps, or hand-drawn place cards. Simple and stylish, it's a scheme that's well suited to a family lunch or dinner with friends.

prints and patterns *(above) Patterned or printed napkins and napkin ties can work well with this theme too, as long as they are in keeping with the cool colour palette.*

base notes *(left) Keep the tabletop tones dark and moody for an unfussy, masculine effect. Grey, purple and blue tones will create a simple backdrop; use the table linen and napkins to add splashes of rich colour and quirky graphic details that will bring the look to life.*

perfect points

Precise pleats add a chic, tailored effect to any setting. To achieve a crisp finish, it is vital that you use cotton or linen napkins and that you starch them well before you start, otherwise they will not be stiff enough to hold their folds. Grey or beige creates a sophisticated yet natural effect.

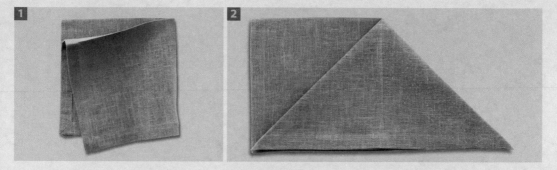

one Press and spray starch an open, square napkin and fold into quarters.

two Holding the napkin with the fold to the right, lift the left-hand corner top layer and pull it out towards the right to make a triangle.

three Turn the folded napkin over from left to right.

four Holding the napkin in place, pull the top layer of the bottom right corner towards the left to form a large triangle.

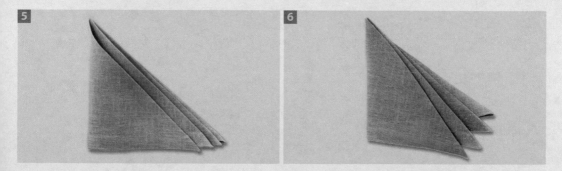

five Fold the triangle in half from left to right.

six Fan out the napkin so that the four points are evenly spaced and lay the napkin on a plate as desired.

diamond

An excellent choice for a sit-down occasion with four or more guests, this fold can be stacked in advance. The napkins don't have to be starched, but choose a fabric that holds a crease. The 'diamond' centre is the perfect place for a name card or bouquet of herbs.

one Make a narrow rectangular strip by folding the bottom third of the napkin upwards and then the top third downwards over the lower third. Holding the centre point of the top edge with your finger, fold half of the strip diagonally downwards.

two Turn the napkin over from left to right so that the folded end is now underneath. Fold one corner of this lower flap inwards and then repeat with the other corner so that the flap forms a triangular point.

three Place your finger at the midpoint of the left-hand diagonal edge of the napkin. With your other hand, fold the triangular flap diagonally right and upwards so that the lower point now forms the right-hand corner of the diamond. To finish, fold the right-hand half of the strip under so that the diamond sits neatly on a square border. Crease the fold with your thumb.

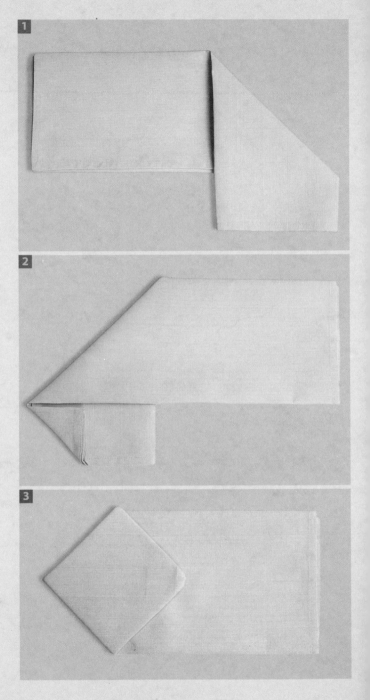

orignial source *(opposite, top left and right)* Chopsticks are a must at any Eastern feast. Look in Asian supermarkets, shop online or collect them on your travels.

beautiful embroidery *(oppposite bottom left)* Handmade in Japan, this raw silk coaster is decorated with a diamond pattern in two colours of silk.

fine fabrics *(opposite, bottom right)* This satin placemat is made from Chinese fabric.

authentic finishing touches *(top right)* A hand-blocked cotton Indian napkin complements a bowl of cardamom seeds, which are traditionally used to freshen the breath.

perfect harmony *(bottom right)* Cultures clash with harmonious results: black Korean dishes, a rice bowl from Vietnam, a brown napkin and wooden napkin ring from Europe, and decorated wooden chopsticks from Japan sit on a Japanese raw silk placemat.

asian fusion

With simple tableware in organic shapes, natural textures and rich colours, an Eastern-themed table is perfect for a sophisticated dinner party. Make use of what you have – plain white dinner plates, stoneware bowls or rush tablemats – then introduce some Eastern elements. Throw a length of fabric across the table and banish knives and forks in favour of chopsticks.

keep it low *(above)* Fun and
informal, low-level dining makes
a change from conventional
entertaining, and a coffee table
or low bench creates the perfect
tabletop. Cover with a length of
colourful fabric and surround it
with a scattering of comfortable
cushions and you'll achieve the
look in an instant.

Eastern style *(above)*
Choosing an Eastern
theme for a dinner party
can give you the chance
to indulge in deep colours,
rich patterns and exotic
textures.

Napkins are not traditionally used in
Eastern cultures. Instead, it has long
been the custom to offer guests small
hot damp towels at the end of a meal.
The use of Eastern-style napkins in
these cultures has been a result of
cross-fertilization. Eastern cuisines were
influenced by Western dining styles and
the practice of using napkins became
more common. Many contemporary
Asian napkins are quite unusual. They
are often fashioned from raw silks or
pigment-dyed linens, which, when
combined with the distinctive pottery
glazes of the East, create a muted
palette of colour that can happily find
a place in any style of table decoration.

oriental ornament *(opposite)*
Genuine tableware makes all the
difference to an Eastern-themed
table. Beautiful tea sets from Japan;
raw silk napkins from China;
porcelain spoons and chopsticks
can be easily obtained
or collected on travels.

bow

The 'bow' is perfect for an Eastern feast and is very easy to make. Try a heavy linen napkin with a graphic pattern to make the most of this fun and stylish napkin fold. A variety of neutral colours and textures work well for both linen and tableware in this theme. Chopsticks can be either tucked into the napkin vertically, underneath the central band, or placed alongside the folded napkin to complete the setting.

one Press and spray starch an open, square napkin. Fold the top and bottom edges of the napkin inwards.

two Fold the bottom edge of the napkin up to meet the top edge, folding it in half.

three Fold the right-hand half of the napkin up towards the centre and the left-hand side of the napkin down towards the centre to form a twist, creasing the folds with your thumb.

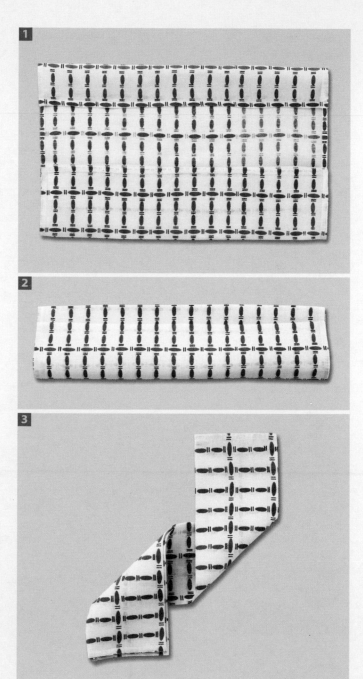

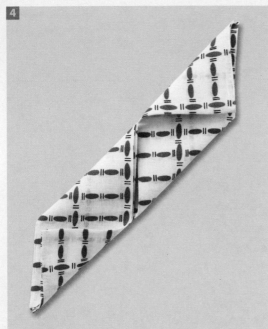

four Fold the top inner corner of each end of the napkin down towards the centre to make a triangle. You should now see four triangles in a line.

five Fold the top triangle down and the bottom triangle up.

six Fold the left and right corners at each end inwards into the centre.

seven Turn the napkin over from left to right. Put your chopsticks through the centre of the bow and display on a plate as desired.

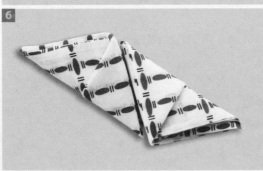

all in the detail *Hydrangea sprigs have been wired onto these classic silver napkin rings to echo the pink and green colour combination of the tabletop flowers.*

adding interest *(opposite)* *This scheme is the perfect example of how texture and colour can bring a table to life. Vibrant touches of pink and green lift the calm, neutral tones of the room, while textured papers and fabrics add subtle pattern to the scene.*

pure elegance *(below)* *A crisply starched, freshly laundered napkin in white or cream is an indispensable adornment to your table. It will add gravitas and style to any dining experience. If you are skilful with a needle, try stitching a monogram in white thread on white fabric so that it almost looks embossed.*

classic elegance

For a special occasion, pull out all the stops and dress your table up to the nines. You don't need fine china and crystal glasses (though if you have them, make the most of them) – the key to a beautiful table is how you dress it. Getting the background right makes all the difference: polish the table, buff up the dining chairs and throw on a beautiful cloth or runner. Then choose a colour scheme – a delicate, pastel palette is best for classic elegance.

water lily

One of the best-known folds, and a favourite with children who make it from paper to create a fortune-telling game, the 'water lily' is equally suitable for both formal and informal occasions. If you want a flat, open lily, use napkins made of soft, unstarched cloth; a crisper fabric will create sharper edges and a taller, bowl-like shape.

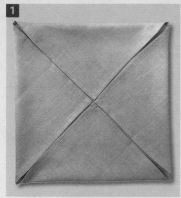

one First find the exact centre of the napkin. Fold it in half to form a rectangle and crease the fold with your thumb. Open out and repeat the fold the other way. The point at which the folds meet is the centre. Fold each of the corners in so that they meet at the centre to form a square.

two Now fold one corner in again, making sure that the point is exactly in the centre of the napkin.

three Fold the other three corners into the centre so that you form a smaller square. Crease all the folds with your thumb.

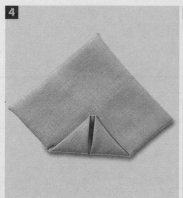

four Carefully lift the napkin and turn it over from left to right, keeping all of the folded corners tucked flat underneath. Now fold one of the corners into the centre.

five Fold each of the other three corners into the centre in the same way so that you once again form a square.

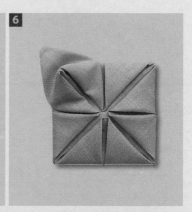

six Carefully holding the points at the centre with your fingers, gently pull out the flap from under one of the corners. Pull out the other corners in the same way.

petal

The 'petal' is among the prettiest of all napkin folds. Perfect for an ornate and elegant setting, this fold mimics the layers of petals of a flower. Pale pastel pinks, blues or lilacs are the obvious colour choices, and you can even use two different shades to create a pretty, layered effect as seen here. Make sure you starch the fabric before folding so that the petals hold their shape on the table.

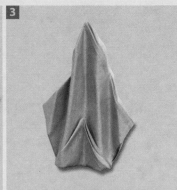

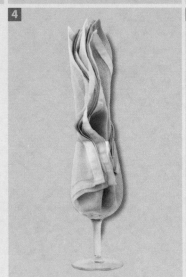

one Press and spray starch an open, square napkin. Fold the napkin into quarters, placing the four loose corners on the right.

two Fold the bottom corner of the napkin up one third.

three Accordion-pleat the folded napkin from the left side corner to the right side corner.

four Put the bottom of the napkin into a wine glass.

five Separate the napkin layers, shaping as desired to look like pretty petals.

vintage charm

Nothing can beat the charm of an old-fashioned tea table laden with delicious things to eat, and it couldn't be simpler to achieve. The ingredients? A simple white linen cloth piled high with frills, florals and fairy cakes. It doesn't matter if nothing matches — that's all part of the quirky vintage appeal.

tea party tabletop
With a nostalgic nod to your grandmother's tea table, introduce frills, flowers and chintzy china for your vintage tea party. Don't forget to offer aromatic Earl Grey tea and delicious cakes and biscuits / cookies.

pretty old-fashioned *(left and far left) A vintage tea party is the perfect occasion for making the most of pretty traditional tableware. Sprigged porcelain tea cups and plates fit the bill perfectly. Keep the colours pale and pretty — faded pinks, delicate lilacs and soft blues, set against white or cream — and favour curved shapes over straight lines. Fresh flowers displayed in vases or tea cups are charming in this vintage setting.*

flowers and frills *(right) Pretty napkins edged with lace are perfect for this theme. Add fresh flowers to each setting to complete the look.*

vintage decoration *(below left) A lace-edged embroidered handkerchief doubles as a napkin in a delicate hand-painted tea cup.*

adding interest *(below left)* The matching rose-patterned tablecloth and napkin are separated by vintage creamware with a delicate edge pattern. A simple cloth ring saves the setting from being too busy.

pure elegance *(below right)* A crisply starched, freshly laundered napkin in white or cream with scalloped or lace edges is perfect for this feminine theme. For an elegant touch, try adding a delicately embroidered napkin ring.

simplicity is perfection *(above)* Crisply starched napkins don't need much dressing up to look elegant. Simple folds and napkin rings are all you need.

all that glitters *(below)* Add a touch of sparkle to your napkins by adding decorative pieces of vintage-style jewellery to napkin rings. Props can also be used to create a talking point for guests.

You can find everything you need for a beautiful, vintage-themed table without looking very far. Start by rummaging in your cupboards to find white, cream or pastel-coloured table linen. Junk shops and thrift stores are great for picking up interesting pieces of tableware and decorations for trimming or tying napkins. Haberdashery sections in department stores also tend to stock a wealth of pretty, vintage-style embellishments for napkins, as well as other finishing touches such as cake stands and doilies.

vintage haberdashery *Ivory linen napkins are folded and held in place by vintage cotton upholstery trims, fastened like a belt. The pristine 1940s upholstery rings, perfectly matching the woven trims, were discovered in a street market in their original unopened haberdasher's packet.*

ruffles

This dainty, delicate fold is ideal for a vintage tea party setting. A starched linen napkin is best for this fold, as it is necessary that the pleats remain sharp and hold the shape of the fan. Choose sugar pinks, pale lilacs, knocked-back blues or other faded shades to complement vintage-style tableware. Tie the napkin with a pretty ribbon in a matching colour to complete the setting.

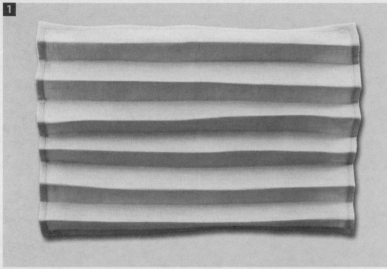

one Press and spray starch an open, square napkin and accordion-pleat the napkin from the bottom edge to the top edge. Starch and iron each crease as you fold so that the pleats are stiff enough to stand up like a concertina when the napkin is flat. Continue this way until the whole rectangle is pleated in sharp folds.

two Fold the pleated napkin in half, holding the pleats securely in place at both ends.

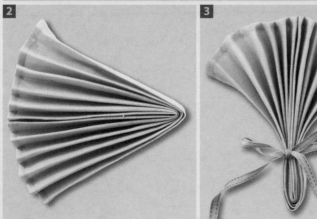

three Tie a ribbon around the fold, about 5 cm/2 inches from the bottom of the napkin, and fan out the pleats at the top. Display the napkin on a plate as desired.

bouquet

This very simple fold works well with a floral-patterned napkin in a light, delicate fabric. There is no need to starch the napkin for this fold, as the desired effect is light and soft, rather than crisp. If using a floral fabric, opt for plain tableware in white, cream or pale pastel hues. A simple napkin ring is a good choice here so as not to distract from the napkin itself.

one First find the exact centre of the napkin. Grasp the centre between your fingers and let the rest of the napkin hang loosely.

two Slide the pointed end of the napkin through a napkin ring until the napkin ring is about 5 cm/2 inches from the bottom.

three Shape the folds of the napkin into a pretty bouquet shape and display on a plate as desired.

white on white

The most traditional napkins for formal occasions
are white damask or linen — freshly laundered, crisply
starched and set on a perfectly folded tablecloth with
a sharp crease that runs vertically along the centre of
the table. Once table linens were kept in linen presses
in order to keep the folds as sharp as possible.

The formal white napkin has a long history
and when used in times past it was an important
sign that they were clean and undefiled. White
napkins for our most auspicious occasions should
be generous — the bigger the better — and can,
because of their crispness, be folded to augment
the full effect of a wonderfully inviting tablescape
gleaming with glass, silver and linens.

understated elegance *Create an elegant,
formal setting using crisp, white table linen
matched with white tableware. Decorate the
table with plenty of fresh flowers.*

variations on a theme *A shell threaded onto ribbon; a button on ribbon; and a satin-bound pipe cleaner clasping a single perfect pearl are three variations of napkin ties perfect for this theme.*

decorative details *A corner of the pristine white napkin emerges from the neat coil exactly fitting the bowl, adding interest to this white-on-white place setting.*

traditional monograms *This wonderful collection of French damask cotton and damask linen napkins with hand-embroidered monogrammes dates from between 1880 and 1920.*

formal setting *In keeping with the precision and formality of the table setting, the chairs are lined up down one side of the top table. In the background, the cake sits on a long, white shelf.*

fan

The 'fan' is a favourite of many restaurants and is easy to make. It requires heavy damask cotton or linen napkins to make the most of the pleated effect. The rear 'tail' serves to anchor the fan on the plate.

one Starching is essential for this fold otherwise the fan will not stand upright. Spray starch the entire napkin before you start, and then fold the napkin in half to form a rectangle. To create the fan effect, start to pleat from one of the short ends of the rectangle in even, equally sized folds; each fold should be approximately 2.5 cm/1 inch wide. Starch and iron each crease as you fold so that the pleats are stiff enough to stand upright like a concertina when the napkin is flat. Continue in this way until half the rectangle is pleated in sharp folds.

two Fold the napkin in half lengthways. The pleats should be on the outside of the fold so that they can fan out, and the open edge of the napkin should be at the top.

three Fold the unpleated portion of the napkin diagonally upwards to prevent the pleats at the top of the fan from opening up. Fold the bottom strip under the lower edge to form the supporting tail. Finally, fan the pleats out to their full extent.

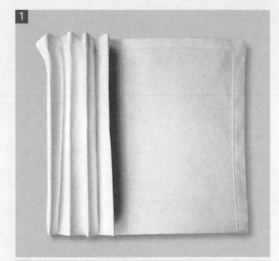

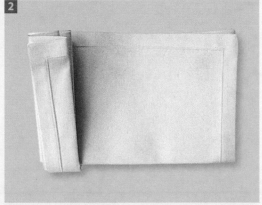

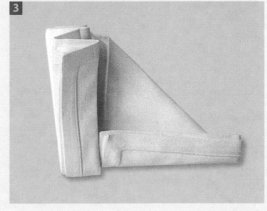

wheatstalk

The 'wheatstalk' requires heavy damask cotton or linen napkins to ensure that it stays upright when folded. This majestic napkin fold is perfect for formal dining. With its smart, clean lines and elegant height, it creates a sense of occasion perfect for a formal get-together. This napkin fold would work well for an anniversary dinner or an engagement party.

one Press and spray starch an open, square napkin. Fold the napkin into quarters, placing the four loose corners at the top. Fold the bottom corner to lie about 5 cm/2 inches beneath the top corner.

two Turn the napkin over from left to right.

three Fold the side corners inwards, overlapping one in front of the other. Tuck the top corner into the pocket of the other corner. Round out the napkin and display on a plate as desired.

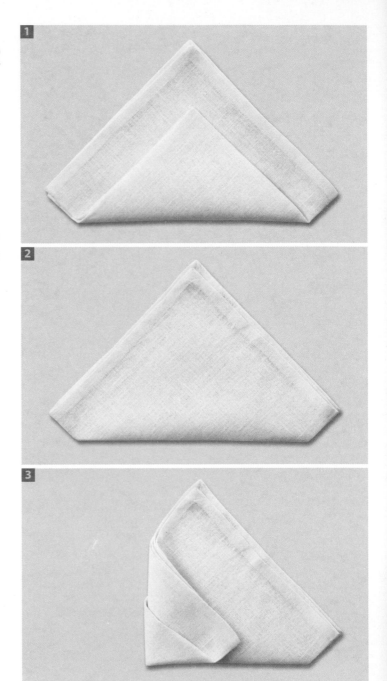

all that glitters

The festive period is the perfect time for family and friends to get together. The prettiest festive tables are simply dressed and inviting, so prepare in advance and keep it simple. Warm, cosy textures, rich colours and sparkling candlelight are all you need to create a beautifully decorated table for all the family to enjoy.

decorative details *Add a touch of sparkle to your festive table with candles and homemade table decorations. Gold and silver always work well in a festive setting, and lots of candles will create an inviting atmosphere for your guests To make these frosted forest table decorations, arrange whitened twigs (available from most florists) in damp floral foam, then conceal the foam beneath a cloud of white feathers (in this case from an old feather boa).*

warm tones *(far right)* This white table setting combines a sense of occasion with a sense of fun. There's a slightly festive overtone, but the simple china and the limited colour palette keep it subtle and stylish.

festive foliage *(right)* Tie napkins with flexible twigs (thin birch twigs are ideal), then tuck in a sprig of evergreen foliage and snowberries. Arrange the napkins in a basket with pine cones and greenery.

pretty patterns *(above and right)* The muted tartan runner with a brighter trim gives this table setting a traditional feel. The tartan ribbon and anemone flowers are a pretty alternative to napkin rings, and the candles in the centre are surrounded by an unusual combination of ornamental cabbages and more anemones.

cosy christmas table *A simple table can still be festive, so take inspiration from the Scandinavians, who have honed the homespun Christmas look to perfection. Stick to natural colours and textures. An antique linen cloth or a blanket will make a tactile tablecloth.*

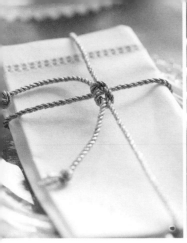

You don't need to buy lots of festive ephemera for the Christmas table. With a little pre-planning, it's easy to rustle up the ingredients for an inviting setting. Track down an antique blanket or a hessian/burlap runner to use as a cloth, then top this with simple, warm-coloured dinnerware and handmade accessories. Get creative and make your own placemats or napkin rings out of coloured felt, pretty ribbons and other festive accessories.

make it personal
(above and below) Crisp damask or linen napkins in white, cream or red work well for holiday entertaining. Add napkin rings and trimmings in seasonal golds and reds to brighten up your table and conjure up a few festive flourishes to make the occasion feel extra special. Personal details such as wrapping individual offerings using the 'festive gift' napkin fold (see overleaf) and having all the napkins monogrammed with your guests' initials, will make them feel particularly welcome.

festive gift

Many hosts like to present a small token to their guests. An effective way to do this is to wrap a small gift in a box in a table napkin. This may be served at the beginning of the evening or brought in, already tied up, before the dessert course, depending on the occasion.

one You will need a large napkin to wrap generously around a box. If you wish the corners to hold their shape, the napkin should be starched or made of a stiffer fabric such as taffeta. Lay the box at an angle to the corners.

two Pick up two opposite corners and bring them together above the box. Roll them down and fold them over the top of the box.

three Fold in the excess fabric on each of the long ends to form narrow strips.

four Carefully pick up the wrapped box and turn it over. Tie up the two ends. The box will now be upside down, so take care that your gift is secure within it. It will be the right way up when your guest unwraps the napkin.

wedding day

Napkins are vital to protect delicate dresses and smart suits from splashes and spills at a wedding, but they also give you an opportunity to use your imagination when deciding how to present them. Choosing the very best-quality napkins will add simple elegance to place settings. Fine linen, starched damask or gauzy organza are all options that work well. Accessories and dressings should be simple but striking, such as garden greenery and lengths of ribbon.

elegant and practical *(above)* *Crisp starched napkins are both beautiful and practical. Fold them to hold breadsticks for each setting, to serve with soup. By using plain white napkins you do not interfere with the chosen colour theme, and a sprig of foliage tucked into the folds adds contrast.*

flawless style *(left)* *For this immaculate white-on-white setting, napkins have been tied in the middle with gold ribbon and draped over the plates. The place cards sit above and just to the left of each plate, held in silver card holders.*

the big day *A well-laid table is a visual pleasure; it not only looks inviting but it makes guests feel welcome. Napkins are folded in half, then into three, and set in the centre of each diner's plate (they may also be set on the left-hand side). Small bunches of hand-picked roses add a personal touch to the occasion.*

Tablecloths and napkins for a wedding table can be cotton, linen or a man-made mixture and come in a variety of weaves or finishes, the classic choice being damask. Table linen can be hired in a rainbow of colours as well as whites, ivories and creams. A neutral backdrop is the easiest to work with, but coloured napkins can look very pretty, particularly if one or two pastel shades are contrasted with a white cloth. For extra interest on the table, cloths can be layered. Alternatively, runners can be placed over tablecloths to add texture, pattern and colour.

dazzling decorations *(opposite, all)* *A stylish but simple twist of ribbon, a piece of inexpensive jewellery or a place card tucked into a napkin ring are just a few ways you can decorate and adorn napkins for your wedding table.*

focal points *(below)* *Bring your wedding table to life by adding a floral focal point. Flowers are the obvious choice, but foliage arrangements can be striking too. Add a personal touch with individual bouquets for each of your guests.*

sheer exuberance *(above)* *The arrangement of a sheer napkin emerging from an empty wine glass gives a playful yet stylish effect.*

fleur de lys

The 'fleur de lys' napkin fold echoes the shape of the historic fleur de lys — a stylized lily or iris that is widely used as a decorative design or symbol. It has appeared on many coats of arms and flags, and is particularly associated with the French monarchy. Use starched linen so that the pointed top and outer petals retain their majestic shape. This smart floral fold is perfect for a garden-themed table.

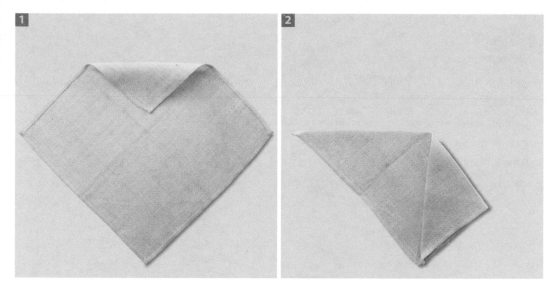

one Press and spray starch an open, square napkin. Fold it in half on the diagonal, bringing the top corner down to the bottom corner to make a large triangle.

two Fold the pointed side corners down to meet the bottom corner.

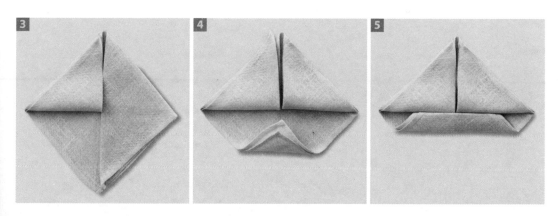

three Fold the same pointed corners up to the top corner.

four Fold the bottom pointed corners up to meet the centre of the napkin.

five Fold the bottom folded edge up to the centre of the napkin to form a band.

six Fold the band just formed up so that it is just above the centre of the napkin.

seven Carefully turn the folded napkin over from left to right.

eight Fold the left-hand corner of the napkin one third inwards towards the right.

nine Tuck the right-hand corner in between the folds of the opposite corner to form a pocket.

ten Round out the base of the folded napkin so that it stands neatly upright.

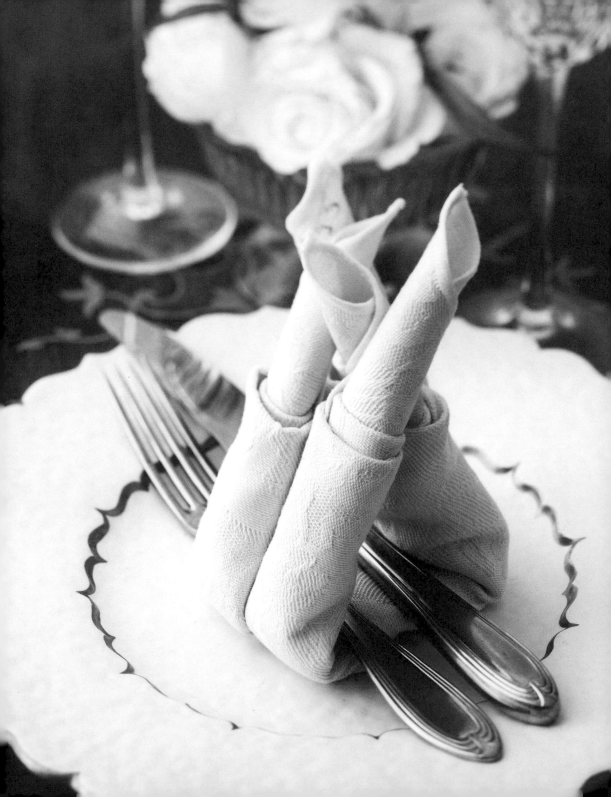

guard of honour

Folding napkins into tall shapes is an ingenious way of adding a vertical dimension to a table arrangement. To achieve a crisp finish, it is vital that you use cotton or linen napkins and that you starch them well before you start, otherwise they will not be stiff enough to stand upright.

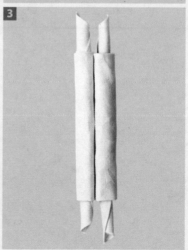

one The larger the napkin you use, the taller your finished design will be. First fold the napkin in half to form a rectangle. Crease the fold with your thumb and then open out the napkin again so that it is flat. Fold the top and bottom halves of the napkin into the middle so that the edges meet at the creased centre line. Holding the two edges together at the centre point of the napkin with your fingers, fold back each corner in turn at an angle so that you form a flat windmill shape.

two Starting at one of the short ends, roll up the napkin tightly until you reach the central point. Place something heavy on the rolled side to keep it in place, or it may spring back.

three Roll the second half tightly into the centre to meet the other roll. Pick up the napkin and bend the rolled napkin so that the ends slot through each other. Place a knife and fork though the base of the napkin to anchor it in place and to prevent the ends from springing outwards.

mood lighting *(left)* *Use sparkling candles in gleaming holders to enhance the atmosphere. Now turn off the overhead lights and let dusk fall…*

a touch of romance *(left) An engagement ring makes a charming napkin clasp for a romantic anniversary dinner for two.*

opulent decorations *(below left) Squares of linen are hemmed to make napkins, each with a faceted copper button at one corner.*

luxurious fabrics *(below) Use a richly patterned cloth covered with accessories in jewelled colours to enhance the mood. These chocolate-coloured napkins tied with ornate brocade ribbon are perfect for this theme.*

romantic opulence

Even the simplest table can be dressed up for a romantic dinner. Create drama with dark, jewelled colours and low-level lighting, use tactile dinnerware and sparkling, ornate glass, then add a dash of glamorous gold. Against this seductive background, serve luxurious, sensual food: soft fresh figs, succulent strawberries or dark chocolate mousse. And the flowers? Red roses, of course.

a table for two *As there are only two place settings, there is plenty of room on the table for glitz and glamour.*

boat

The 'boat' is a majestic and ornate fold that can add an extra layer of luxury to the occasion. Starched linen napkins in strong plain colours are best to show off the construction of this fold. It is also a large fold, so be sure to use large napkins to ensure that there is enough fabric.

one First press and starch the napkin. Fold the napkin in half and then in half again to form a square a quarter of the size of the open napkin. Fold this square in half diagonally to form a triangle. Position the napkin with the point of the triangle at the top, with the loose corners rather than the folded corners uppermost.

two Holding the topmost point, fold both two sides downwards so that the corners lie below the folded edge of the napkin.

three Turn the napkin over from left to right. Fold one of the lower points upwards over the folded line. Repeat with the other fold so that you have a tall triangular shape.

four Fold both sides together with the folds on the inside and then turn the napkin over so that it sits on the base formed by the bulky tucks. To form the sails for the finished boat, pull each of the loose points up in graduated amounts.

tropical oasis

There's something special about a tropical themed party. It lends a fun and informal air to any occasion and is perfect for dining outdoors. Whether you have a roof terrace, a tiny backyard or a rambling country garden, alfresco entertaining can be the perfect solution for a summer lunch party, and dressing the table couldn't be easier. Keep the look pared down but pretty with simple china, decorative glassware and plenty of fresh flowers.

bold brights *(above)*
Vibrant colours add fun and zest to table settings.

pretty patterns *(left)*
Bright, floral prints are perfect for this exotic theme. Try serving sorbet with printed napkins to create a tropical treat for your guests.

cocktail napkins
(right) Colourful Japanese handkerchiefs are ideal as small cocktail napkins.

in the pink *Outdoor entertaining gives you the opportunity to make the most of your garden. Use the colours around you as inspiration for the tabletop scheme. Here, the brilliant pink of a bold feature wall is repeated in the napkins and the table flowers to create a vibrant and colourful table.*

bird of paradise

This classic, origami-inspired napkin fold works well using a bold, patterned fabric with lots of starch to hold the wings of the bird in place. The 'bird of paradise' is suitable for an informal lunch party and will wow your friends and dinner guests with its exotic, decorative style.

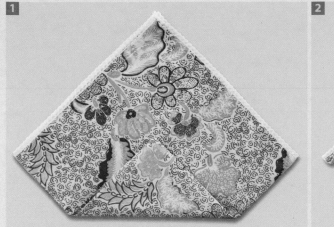

one Press and spray starch an open, square napkin. Fold the napkin into quarters, placing the four loose corners at the bottom. Fold the bottom corner up to the top corner to form a triangle. Crease the folds with your thumb.

two Fold the side edges into the centre of the napkin and crease the folds with your thumb.

three Fold the two bottom corners back underneath the rear edge.

four Fold the napkin in half, bringing the left half behind the right half.

five Holding the bottom end of the napkin in place, pull the loose corners up one by one, fanning them out as you go. Display on a plate as desired.

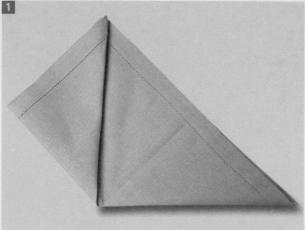

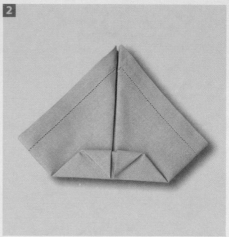

one Press and spray starch the napkin, then fold it in half diagonally to form a triangle. With the folded edge of the triangle nearest to you, fold one corner of the triangle up to the top point. Fold the other corner up to meet it exactly so that you form a square with one corner pointing downwards, with a vertical seam where the two edges meet.

two Fold the bottom corner of the square up and then fold it back down on itself so that the tip of the corner sits exactly on the bottom edge and the vertical seams are aligning. Crease the folds with your thumb.

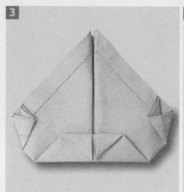

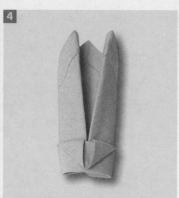

three Fold the left-hand corner inwards, open it out by inserting your finger in it and then press it flat to form a kite shape. Press open the right-hand corner in the same way.

four Pick up the napkin, wrap the two corners around to the back and tuck them into each other. The turned-back corners will help to support the napkin and give it a strong tubular shape when it is standing upright.

five Bend down the two loose points and, to secure them, tuck their tips into the turn-up at the bottom. Do not crease the fold; a soft curve will give a more pleasing effect.

french lily

An advanced, lofty fold, the 'French lily' can create a quite spectacular effect as it sits extremely high upon the plate. It suits a flamboyant and festive occasion.

practical style *(left)*
Two checked napkins wrapped around ice cream cones add to the fun of an outdoor party and will always come in handy later for the inevitable meltdown.

pretty special *(below)*
Choose a wicker hamper to carry everything you need for the day and wrap essential items in napkins secured with a pretty bow to protect them in transit.

rustic checks *(below)*
A jaunty rustic check is an ideal napkin for wrapping a casual lunch.

nostalgic charm *(below)*
A classic French cotton checked napkin has a familiar nostalgic charm.

the great outdoors

Just because you're eating outdoors doesn't mean you can't make an occasion of it. With a little thought and effort, you can turn an impromptu picnic into a memorable event. First choose the perfect spot, then spread out a soft rug on the grass and frame the area with a floaty fabric canopy. A few branches, a length of muslin and a bit of daisy-chain decoration will transform a corner of the park into your own little oasis.

pocket

The 'pocket' is best suited to outdoor dining as the cutlery/flatware can be neatly tucked away inside the folds. Use this stylish and practical fold for a barbecue or picnic. A fun, checked fabric in a shade to match your colour scheme is the perfect choice to achieve a stylish outdoor feel.

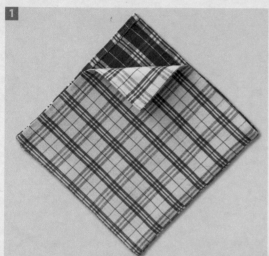

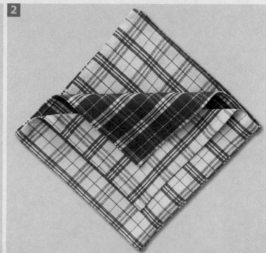

one Press and spray starch an open, square napkin. Fold the napkin into quarters, placing the four loose corners at the top. Fold the first layer of the top corner down to just above the bottom corner.

two Fold the next layer from the top corner down so that it is just above the last layer.

three Fold both side corners underneath the napkin, creasing the folds with your thumb and making sure that both sides are even. Tuck a knife and fork inside the pocket and display on the plate as desired.

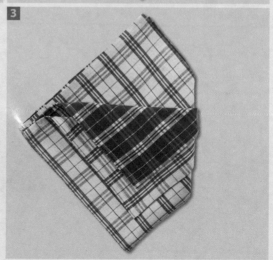

coastal table style

On a warm summer's day, what could be better than an impromptu barbecue? It won't need much planning and can be far more convivial than a sit-down dinner party. Make sure you have plenty of comfortable seating, and enough lighting if it's an evening event. Why not try a decorative theme for the tabletop, such as this coastal-inspired style. It's easy to put together and looks fantastic.

carry on camping *(below)* Sturdy camping tins make inspired serving dishes for bread, fruit or even cutlery / flatware and add to the informal, outdoorsy feel.

ocean blues *(below)* These napkins made from men's shirting stripes add a touch of humour. Striped blues suit white plates and a blue tablecloth.

seaside stripes *(below)* A pair of striped dish towels can be cut up and made into a set of napkins. Look for the rims of shells on seaside walks for a natural napkin ring.

plain sailing *A bright and breezy nautical theme is ideal for a barbecue and is also easy to assemble. Throw on a stripy cloth, pile food and cutlery into camping containers and use rope and mini sailing clasps for napkin ties (most ship chandlers should stock a wide selection).*

lantern light *(above) Use plenty of candles on the table at an evening barbecue to make sure you have enough light.*

tuxedo

The 'tuxedo' is a smart fold and very easy to master. It is particularly useful for buffets or occasions at which guests will receive their cutlery/flatware and napkin in one go, and for elegant picnics or fêtes champêtres where the cutlery provides an anchor for the table linen. A place name card or sweet herbs may also be tucked into one of the folds for a personal touch. This fold works best on a large plain napkin that is perfectly square. For best results and a really crisp edge, press and spray starch the napkins before you begin.

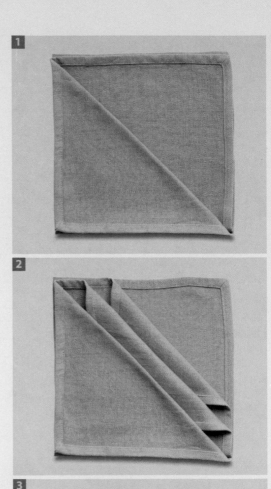

one Fold the napkin in half and then in half again to form a square a quarter of the size of the open napkin. (If you are going to use the folded napkin to hold cutlery, check at this point that the handles are not too long for the napkin; if they are you will have to use larger napkins.) With the open corners positioned at the top right, fold the top layer back over the opposite corner so that it forms a triangle.

two Fold back each of the next two layers in turn. Don't fold them back all the way – instead, tuck the corner of each under the previous fold so that you form a rippled effect. When you are happy with the proportions, press the folds flat with your thumb.

three Fold the right-hand third of the napkin to the back, including all folded layers. To finish, fold the left-hand third under and then slide your cutlery/flatware or other decoration into the fold.

the settings

Don't fret too much about etiquette or conventions
when it comes to table settings. The intention is simply
to provide the diner with the right tools in the right place
for whatever dishes are on the menu. This chapter looks
at a few classic formations to get you started.

international informal

This basic table setting will work for any informal Western meal and can be adapted depending on the food being served. Cutlery/flatware is positioned in the most convenient place for the diner: dinner fork to the left of the dinner plate; knives and soup spoons to the right and dessert forks and spoons above the plate, with handles facing the hand that will be using them. The glasses are positioned at the top right, with the largest glass (generally the red wine glass) set at the back for neatness.

1 Napkin in a simple fold
2 Dinner fork
3 Dinner plate
4 Dinner knife
5 Soup spoon

6 Dessert spoon
7 Dessert fork
8 White wine glass
9 Red wine glass
10 Water glass

British formal

For a dinner party, you may want to use a more formal table setting involving a wider selection of tableware. In this case, all the cutlery/flatware for the meal can be placed either side of the dinner plate and should be laid from the outside in so that the first-course cutlery/flatware is outermost (and thus most accessible) and the dessert spoon and fork innermost. A side plate for bread can be set to the left, and if you want to supply a butter knife, this can be laid across the plate in line with the edge of the table.

1 Napkin in a simple fold
2 Side plate
3 Dinner fork
4 Dessert fork
5 Dinner plate
6 Dessert spoon

7 Dinner knife
8 Soup spoon
9 White wine glass
10 Red wine glass
11 Water glass

English afternoon tea

If you are serving a formal sit-down tea, make sure you provide appropriate utensils for whatever food you are offering. You may need a butter knife, a pastry fork and even a spoon for a particularly creamy cake. These implements should all be set to the right of the plate, with the napkin placed on the left (or on top of the plate if you prefer). For a proper afternoon tea, it's imperative to use your very best teacups and saucers; mugs just won't give you the same sense of occasion.

1 Napkin in a simple fold
2 Side plate
3 Bread knife
4 Dessert spoon
5 Pastry fork
6 Saucer
7 Teacup
8 Teaspoon

American formal

Very similar to the British formal style, the American setting also places cutlery/flatware for each course either side of the dinner plate, working from the outside in. Here, the first course is a fish dish, so the outermost items are a fish knife and fork. Cutlery/flatware for the main course and dessert then follow. Americans tend to place bread or salad plates to the top left of the setting rather than at the side. Glasses are set in the standard triangular formation.

1 Napkin in a simple fold
2 Fish fork
3 Dinner fork
4 Dessert fork
5 Dinner plate
6 Dessert spoon
7 Dinner knife
8 Fish knife
9 White wine glass
10 Red wine glass
11 Water glass
12 Bread or salad plate

French formal

Unlike the British and Americans, the French place their cutlery/flatware face down on the table and use a tablespoon for soup instead of a rounded soup spoon. Side plates and butter knives are not required, as bread is placed directly on the table and butter is not generally served. Cutlery/flatware is laid out in a standard Western style, but a knife rest is sometimes used so that the dinner knife can be laid back on the table and reused for the cheese course, which in France is served before the dessert.

1 Napkin in a simple fold
2 Dinner fork
3 Dessert fork
4 Dinner plate
5 Dessert spoon
6 Dinner knife
7 Soup spoon
8 White wine glass
9 Red wine glass
10 Water glass

Chinese informal

A standard Western dinner plate, side plate and bowl can just as easily form part of a Chinese table setting, but a few extra accessories will be required to finish it off. You'll need a handleless teacup for jasmine or green tea; a Chinese soup spoon (ideally one that matches the bowl); a little dish for dipping sauces; chopsitcks and a chopstick stand. You may also need an extra rice bowl if you are serving both soup and rice, but this can be brought to the table as needed. And conventional cutlery/flatware should be available for guests who are inexperienced with chopsticks.

1 Dinner plate
2 Chopsticks
3 Chopstick stand
4 Sauce dish
5 Tea cup
6 Soup bowl
7 Soup spoon
8 Saucer

Japanese informal

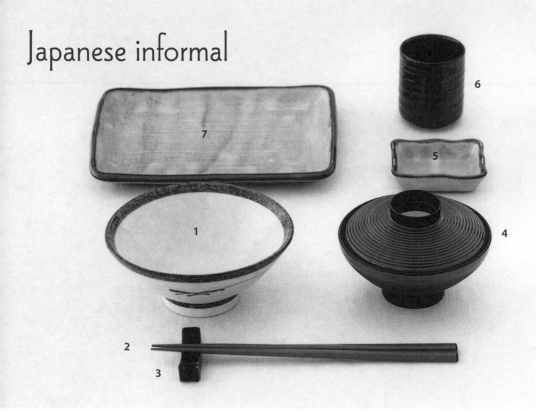

Much like the Chinese setting, the Japanese table requires a number of bowls, dishes and plates for serving all the elements of a Japanese meal. Rice, noodles and soups are served in a bowl; sushi and sashimi, fried and grilled dishes are served on an open plate. Small dishes are needed for sauces and pickles, and a handleless teacup for miso soup. A small jug can also be used for soy sauce so that guests can help themselves. Chopsticks should be positioned right at the front of the setting with the ends pointing towards the left.

1 Rice bowl
2 Chopsticks
3 Chopstick stand
4 Soup bowl
5 Pickle dish
6 Tea cup
7 Dinner plate

index

picture credits

KEY: a = above,
b = below, r = right,
l = left, c = centre.

endpapers by
David Loftus

Caroline Arber
pages 13 al, 56 bl, 57,
71 al and bc, 84 ac

Carolyn Barber
pages 8, 26–27, 36–37,
44–47, 52–53, 58–62,
66–67, 78–80, 90–91,
96–97

Martin Brigdale
page 35 r

David Brittain
pages 2, 103–109

Lisa Cohen
pages 20, 31 al and bl

Sandra Lane
pages 13 br, 56 al, 69 al
and ar, 71 ar

William Lingwood
pages 28–29, 32–33,
72, 82–83, 100–101

David Loftus
pages 6 inset, 7, 9–11,
13 ar and bl, 14–16,
17 ar, 18–19, 21, 24 r,
38–41, 42 b, 48 ac and
ar, 50–51, 55 bl, 63 ac

and ar, 64–65, 73, 75,
81, 84 ar, 86–87, 88 bl
and br, 92–94, 98 bc

Paul Massey
pages 30 r, 31 br, 84 al

Mark Scott
page 98 br

Lucinda Symons
page 56 c

Debi Treloar
pages 4, 5 al and bl, 6
background, 12, 13 ac,
17 al, 17 bl, 17 br,
22–23, 25, 30 l, 31 ar,
34, 35 l, 42 a, 43, 48 al
and bl, 49, 54, 55 al, 55
ar, 55 br, 70, 84 br, 85,
88 al, 89, 95, 98 bl and
ar, 99, 102

Jo Tyler
pages 68, 69 bl and br,
71 bl & br

Polly Wreford
pages 1, 3, 5 ar and br,
24 l, 56 r, 63
background, 63 al, 71
ac, 74, 76–77